Ole

MW00425079

Joke Book

"It Could Be Worse"

Written and Compiled by
Mary E. Hirsch

Copyright 2019 by Mary E Hirsch

All rights reserved

It is the property of Mary E. Hirsch who is
a Minnesotan and so it is protected by the
Gods of Norway, Sweden, Finland, Denmark,
Iceland and a few other cold places.

Published in the United States by Mary E. Hirsch

www.swellthoughts.com

First Edition

Dedicated to all the faithful readers
of Ingebretsen's Nordic Market's
Sunday Funnies on Facebook.

You inspired (well forced) me to seek out
more and more jokes and to write my own.

And of course dedicated to my family because
I don't want to get to a gathering and have to
be asked why it wasn't dedicated to them.

And to my great-great-grandpa Marcus
Thrane and great-great-grandma
Josephine Thrane -- Norwegian rebels and
rabblerousers!!! Thanks for the great genes.

Introduction

A Few Words about Ole & Lena
And This Here Book
(Because Scandinavians Are People Of
Few Words Don'tcha Know)

I grew up hearing jokes about Ole and Lena, or Ole and Sven, or Ole and Lars and Sven – well you get the picture. I can't say I understood them, but I sure did hear them especially on 'CCO radio and I remember my Uncle Phil loved to tell them too.

They have stood the test of time and are still popular today. Every once in a while I hear someone mention that it is amazing that in this day of political correctness that Norwegians and Swedes and other Scandihoovians aren't offended by the jokes. I think even if we are offended we know better than to say anything and instead just eat about a dozen or so bars until our feelings have been duly suppressed (like all feelings should be).

I don't think Ole and Lena and the gang offends anyone because they are not mean spirited. Every once in a while you'll find a collection with jokes about those dumb Norwegians or stupid Swedes or idiotic Finns (I have yet to see a derogatory joke about the Danish or Icelanders) but that's a different kind of joke and one you won't find here.

When I started posting Ole & Lena jokes on the Facebook page of Ingebretsen's Nordic Market I found the jokes online. There are literally hundreds of sites that have Ole & Lena jokes. Then I started to write my own based on a punch line I heard somewhere or even a t-shirt I saw someone wearing or just a random thought that came into my head. While I have copyrighted this book because I don't want anyone to copy the whole thing and call it their own, I know many of these jokes have been around the block for decades and no one really knows who started them. I'm proud to add the ones that I've written to the mix.

Finally, many sites feature jokes that have translated English to Scandihoovian such as changing "W" to "V" and "Th" to "D" where "Well" becomes "Vel" and "That" becomes "Dat." I have chosen not to translate the word unless it is important to the joke. I did it for a couple of reasons but the two main ones are: it is hard to be consistent with my dis and dats and also it was blowing up my spellchecker!!!!! This means you are responsible for inflecting and interjecting your own dialect.

So, (this introduction is like a long Midwestern good-bye) I guess that's it. Hope you like the book. I still have more jokes so there may be another book or two in the future.

Oops, I almost forgot, the pictures are all copyright free photos from various sources. They just reminded me of Ole, Lena, Sven and company so here they are. Okay, that's about it then.

Ole was on his death bed, The doctor had told
Lena he wouldn't last the night. and he might as
well die at home in his own bed. After a while
Ole's eyes flickered open and he sniffed the air and
smelled lefse baking. He started muttering "lefse
oh lefse."

He pulled himself to the edge of the bed and
slipped to the floor, being too weak to even stand.
Sniffing the air and muttering "lefse oh lefse" he
crawled to the stairs and crawled/fell downstairs.
"Oh lefse" he muttered as he crawled to the
kitchen door.

There he saw his beautiful Lena standing at the
stove making lefse with a stack of finished ones on
the table behind her. He crawled to the table and,
despite the pain, he pulled himself up on a chair
murmuring "oh lefse." He was reaching out for one
when Lena turned and saw him. She smacked his
hand with the spatula and said "Now Ole stop that,
those are for after the funeral."

***

Three sailors, Ole, Sven and Lars, are
shipwrecked and wash up on the coast of a
country in the middle of a guerrilla war. Rebel
forces capture them, put them on trial and
condemns them to death as spies.

The next morning at dawn, Ole is put before the
firing squad. As they take aim he shouts, "TIDAL

WAVE!!!" The troops panic, scatter to higher ground and Ole escapes.

Lars is taken out the next morning. Having heard about Ole from the guards, at the appropriate time he shouts, "EARTHQUAKE!!!" Again the firing squad panics and he escapes.

Sven, when his turn comes, had heard about Ole and Lars but realizes that the firing squad will not fall for the same disaster twice, so he shouts "FIRE!!!"

***

Ole and Lena are having problems remembering things, so they go to the doctor to get checked out. They describe for the doctor the problems they are each having with their memory. After checking them out, the doctor tells them that they are physically okay, but that they might want to start writing things down to help them remember. Ole and Lena thank the doctor and leave.

That night while watching TV, Ole gets up from his chair. Lena asks, "Where are you going?"

Ole replies, "To the kitchen."

"Could you bring me a bowl of ice cream?"

"Sure" Ole answers.

Lena then asks him, "Don't you think you should write it down so you can remember?"

Ole says, "No, I can remember that."

"Well," Lena adds, "then I also would like some strawberries on top. You had better write that down 'cause I know you'll forget." By now Ole is getting mad. "I can remember that you want a bowl of ice cream with strawberries."

"I also would like whipped cream on top. I know you will forget that, so you better write it down," Lena insists.

Obviously irritated Ole says, "I don't need to write that down. I can remember that."

He fumes off into the kitchen. When he returns twenty minutes later he hands her a plate of bacon and eggs. She stares at the plate for a moment and says, "You forgot my toast."

***

So Sven died and went to heaven (yes we are all a little surprised at that). St. Peter said, "Before I let you in, you have to pass a test." "Oh, no!" said Sven, I'm not too smart." St. Peter said, "Don't worry. This is easy. Just answer this question: Who was God's son?" Sven thought for a minute and said, "Andy!" St. Peter said, "Andy?" Sven said "Yah, sure. We sang it in church: 'Andy walks with me, Andy talks with me, Andy tells me I am his own.'"

***

Ole and Lena had married under not so happy circumstances, and their married life had not been anything to brag of either. But when, after thirty-five years of marriage, Ole went to the local judge to ask for an annulment people where shocked. When the hearing came, the judge asked for the reasons why Ole wanted an annulment.

"Here it is," announced Ole, "I just learned that Lena's father never had a license to carry that gun."

***

Ole and Sven were reminiscing about their days in the service.

Ole said "Sven did you know that while I was in the army, I was brought up for an offense."

Sven replied: "Ole I didn't know that, what happened?"

"Well, said Ole, "They gave me the choice of one month's restriction or twenty days' pay. I said, "Okay, I'll take the money."

***

Ole had been ill in the hospital for several months. He kept slipping in and out of a coma but Lena remained faithfully by him every day.

Then one day, when he woke from his coma and saw Lena sitting there, he motioned for her to come nearer to him.

She moved closer and sat beside Ole, her eyes filling with tears as he whispered, "You know

12

what? You've been with me through all the tough times. When I lost my job, you were there to support me. When my business went bankrupt, you were there for me. When I got hit by a car, you were by my side all the time. When we lost the house, you stayed right here with me. And even when my health started failing, you were still by my side... You know what?"

"What dear," Lena asked gently, smiling as her heart began to fill with warmth, her eyes welling with tears.

Ole said, "I think you're bad luck."

***

A hooded robber rushed into a Wisconsin bank and forced the tellers to fill a bag full of cash.

On his way out the door, a brave bank guard grabbed the hood and pulled it off, revealing the robber's face. The robber shot the guard.

The robber looked around the bank and saw one of the tellers looking straight at him. The robber instantly shot him too.

Everyone in the bank, by now terrified, looked down at the floor in silence.

The robber yelled, "Well, did anyone else see my face?"

There were a few moments of silence, everyone was too afraid to speak.

Then, one old Norwegian named Ole from

Minnesota raised his hand and said, "My wife Lena got a pretty good look at you"

***

Ole and Lena are on the patio barbequing when Ole says, "Lena your butt is getting pretty big. It's even bigger than the BBQ grill!"
Lena was not amused.
Later that night in bed, Ole asks Lena, "Say, do you want to, well you know?" Lena turns away and grunts. "What's wrong?" asks Ole.
Lena answers, "Do you really think I'm going to fire-up this big-ass grill for one little weenie?"

***

Ole comes home with Sven and as they walk through the house they notice Lena is in the living room making love to another man. They continue on into the kitchen, and Ole pulls out two beers from the fridge and says, "Here's one for you and one for me." Sven asks, "But what about the guy in the living room?" Ole says, "He can get his own beer."

***

Ole was getting ready to go to work one day when Lena stopped him and complained, "Ole, the washing machine is broke down, don't you know, I want you to fix it!."

Ole walked out the door yelling, "Lena, what do I look like, the Maytag repairman?"

That evening when Ole got home Lena was standing in the yard and said to Ole, "Ole, the car it won't start! Please fix the car."

Ole kept walking into the house yelling, "Lena, what do I look like, Mr. Goodwrench?"

The next day when Ole came home from work Lena said, "Look Ole, the car, is fixed and the washing machine is working too! Lars down the road come by and I asked him if he would fix them for me and he did."

"And what did he charge you for doin' it?" Ole asked. Lena replied, "Well Ole, he said he would do it for some romance (well you know) or if I baked him a cake."

"Well, what kind of a cake did you make him?" asked Ole.

Lena replied, "What do I look like, Betty Crocker?"

***

Ole and Lena are driving at night. Lena starts to worry something is wrong with the blinkers so she pulls over and asks Ole to get out and check them.

"Okay," Ole yells from the front of the car, "It works... Wait it don't work... No now it works... Wait it don't work... No wait, now it works... Oh sorry, it don't work..."

***

Ole walks into a pharmacy and asks the pharmacist for bottom deodorant. "Sorry, we don't sell bottom deodorant" the pharmacist replies, struggling to keep from laughing. "In fact, I have no idea what that is."

"But I always buy it here." Ole says. "I bought one last month."

Thinking quickly, the pharmacist suggests, " I don't know what you bought before, maybe you can bring in the empty container next time."

"Sure," Ole replies. "I'll bring it with me tomorrow."

The next day, Ole walks into the shop again and hands the pharmacist an empty deodorant stick. "This is just a normal deodorant," the pharmacist tells Ole, "You use it under your arms."

"No, it is not," Ole answers, "it says so here: To apply, push up bottom."

***

Lena is watching the news with Ole when the newscaster says, "Six Brazilian men die in a skydiving accident." Lena starts crying to her husband, sobbing, "That's horrible!"

Confused, Ole replies, "Yah sure Lena, that is sad, but there's always a risk with skydiving."

After a minute, Lena, still crying, says, "Ole, how many is a Brazilian?"

***

Ole goes to the doctor and says, "Everywhere I touch with my finger hurts." The doctor asks "What do you mean?"

So Ole shows him what he means. He touches his knee and says "Ouch!" Then he touches his chest and says, "Ouch!" Then he touches his shoulder, "Ouch!"

The doctor looks at Ole and shakes his head. "Ole you dummy, you've got a broken finger!"

***

Ole decides to join a Buddhist monastery as a novice and takes a vow of silence. He's told that once a year he'll have an interview with the head monk when he can say two words. He agrees, and throws himself into his new monastic life, spending time in deep meditation and helping other monks with their tasks.

The first year passes. Ole's called into the head monk's office and asked what he wants to say. Ole replies: "Work . . . hard." The head monk nods and sends him back to the monastery.

Another year passes, and Ole is called into the head monk's office. This time, he says, "Floors . . . cold." The head monk nods and sends him back to the monastery.

The third year passes, and again Ole goes to the head monk's office for an interview. "Well, my son?" the head monk asks. Ole says: "Food . . . bad." The head monk jumps up and exclaims, "I've heard enough, pack your bags and leave."

Ole is stunned. "Why?" he says.

"Why?" the head monk responds. "Because you've done nothing but complain since you got here.

***

Ole's friend Lars stopped by for a visit one day. "How's it going with your marriage, Ole? Is the honeymoon over yet?"

"Well, the marriage is doing fine." said Ole. "And Lena she treats me just like a Greek God."

"That's great," said Lars. "But how are you treated like a Greek God?"

"Well, you see, Lars, every night Lena serves me a burnt offering!"

***

Lena and Helga met at the grocery store. After asking about each other's aches and pains, the conversation turned to their husbands.

"Oh," said Lena, "Ole died. He went out to the garden to dig up a cabbage for dinner don't cha

18

know, had a heart attack, and dropped dead right in the middle of the cabbage patch."

"Oh my!" exclaimed Helga, "What did you do?"

Lena Shrugged, "I came here to buy a cabbage."

***

Lena was trying to get little Sven to eat his carrots. "Now Sven, you better eat them carrots, they're good for your eyes,"

"How do you know?" little Sven asked.

Lena told him, "Have you ever seen a rabbit wearing glasses?"

***

Ole was having trouble with his son, Little Ole, in school. In most classes Little Ole was getting good grades, but in math he was getting a "D." Ole talked with the teacher, but he told Ole that they had tried everything. The principal said the same thing. Both Ole and Lena tutored Little Ole at home, but it didn't help.

Finally, Ole and Lena decided to enroll Little Ole in a parochial school with smaller class sizes hoping he'd get more attention. After three months the report cards came out and Little Ole had gotten an "A" in math! Ole and Lena were proud as could be, but were also quite curious. So they asked, "Little Ole, how did you do it? How did you get an A in math at this school?"

Little Ole replied, "I knew I had to shape up real fast. On the first day at school, we went into the church for morning devotions, and I looked up at the front wall and saw this huge PLUS sign with a man nailed to it. I knew right then this school was really serious about math!"

***

Minnesota's worst air disaster happened when a Cessna 152, a small two-seater plane, crashed into a local Norwegian cemetery yesterday morning.

Ole and Sven, working as search and rescue workers, have recovered 754 bodies so far, and expect that number to climb as digging continues.

***

Ole came home carrying a rock, a chicken, a pail, and two geese, and he asked Lena to open the door for him. She said, "No, I'm afraid you might suddenly want to make love to me." He said, "How could I make love to you with a rock, a chicken, a pail, and two geese in my arms?" "Well," she said, "you could set the chicken down, put the pail over it, then set the rock on top of the pail, and I'll hold the geese."

***

Ole and Sven were fishing one day when Sven pulled out a cigar. Finding he had no matches, he asked Ole for a light.

"Yah, sure, I think I have a lighter," he replied. Then reaching into his tackle box, he pulled out a Bic lighter 10 inches long.

"Jiminy Cricket!" exclaimed Sven, taking the huge Bic lighter in his hands "Where did you get that gigantic lighter??"

"Well," replied Ole, "I got it from my genie."

"You have a genie in your tackle box?" Sven asked.

"Yah, sure It's right here in my tackle box," says Ole.

"Could I see him?"

Ole opens his tackle box and out pops the genie. Talking to the genie, Sven says, "I'm a good friend of your master. Will you grant me one wish?"

"Yes, I will," says the genie.

So Sven asks the genie for a million bucks. The genie disappears back into the tackle box with Sven sitting there, waiting for his million bucks.

All of a sudden, the sky darkens and is filled with the sound of a million ducks flying overhead.

Over the roar of the ducks Sven yells at Ole. "Uff da, I asked for a million bucks, not a million ducks!"

Ole chuckles and says, "Yah, I forgot to tell you

that the genie is hard of hearing. Do you really think I asked for a 10-inch Bic?"

***

Ole and Lena were lying in bed one night when the phone rang, Ole answered it and Lena heard him yell, "Well, how the hell should I know, that's over 2,000 miles away," and he hung up.

Lena said "Who was that Ole?"

Ole said "Hell if I know, some guy wants to know if the coast is clear."

***

Lena was reading Cosmopolitan one day. She turned to Ole and says, "Do you remember if we ever had mutual orgasm?" Ole thought for a minute "Mutual orgasm? No, we always had Allstate."

***

Ole, Sven, and Lars were hiking through a forest in Northern Minnesota when they came upon a raging river. They had to get on the other side so Ole prayed, "God, please give me the strength to cross the river." And just like that, POOF! God gave him big arms and strong legs and he swam across in about two hours, almost drowning twice.

After seeing that, Sven prayed, "God, please give me the strength *and* the tools to cross the river."

And just like that, POOF! God gave him a rowboat and strong arms and strong legs and he rowed across in an hour, almost capsizing once.

Seeing what happened to Ole and Sven, Lars prayed, "God, please give me the strength, the tools *and* the intelligence to cross this river." And just like that, POOF! Lars turned into a woman. She checked the map, hiked one hundred yards upstream, and walked across the bridge.

***

A local DEA agent stops at Ole's farm and tells him, "I have to inspect your fields for marijuana."

"Okie dokie," Ole says, "but you don't to go in that field over there," and points out the location.

The agent explodes, waving his badge and shouting, "Listen, friend. This badge means I can go anywhere I choose, on any land, no questions asked. Get it?"

Ole nods politely, apologizes, and returns to his chores. A short time later, he hears loud screams and sees the agent running for his life, chased by a huge bull. Throwing down his tools Ole runs to the fence, and yells at the top of his lungs, "Your badge! Show him your badge!"

***

Little Ole: Papa, can you help me with my math homework? I have to find the lowest common denominator.

Ole: You mean to tell me they haven't found that yet? They was lookin' for that when I was a boy.

***

Lena: "Ole I had a dream. I saw you in a jewelry store and you bought me a diamond ring."

Ole: "Yah I had the same dream and I saw your dad paying the bill."

***

Ole walked into the kitchen after work and found Lena crying. "What's the matter Lena?" he asked.

"Ole, I baked a cake for you and the dog ate it!" Lena cried.

"That's okay," said Ole, "I'll get you another dog."

***

Ole and Lena were having a big fight. Lena yelled "Ole you never do what I ask you to do."

Ole yelled right back "If I say I'm gonna do something I'll do it" and started walking out the door. He turned back and added "And there is no need to remind me about it every 6 months."

***

Ole was walking along a beach and found a lamp. He rubbed it and a genie appeared and told him, "I will grant you one wish but on one condition; whatever you ask for, your mother-in-law will receive double of the same thing."

Ole thought for a while and said, "Hmmmmmm, all right, give me fifty million dollars and beat me half to death."

***

Sven found Ole sitting in the bar, looking miserable.

"What's the matter Ole?" he asked.

"Well Lena kicked me out and I'm living in the truck." Ole said.

"What happened for goodness sake?" Sven replied.

"Well today's Lena's birthday and this morning she told me 'I just dreamed that you gave me a diamond necklace. What do you think that means?" I told her "Well, maybe you'll find out tonight."

Sven nodded and said "Sooo you got her a diamond necklace right?"

Ole shook his head, "Not quite I got her the book 'The Meaning of Dreams.'"

***

Ole forgot to renew his driver's license so he had to take the test all over again. The State Patrol Officer giving the test tells Ole that when he taps on the dashboard he wants Ole to show what action he'd take if a young child ran out in front of his car. After a few minutes, the Officer taps the dashboard. Ole screeches the car to a halt, puts down the window, and yells to the empty street, "Be careful where you're going, you little jerk!"

***

Lena passed away and Ole called 911. The 911 operator told Ole she'd send someone out right away.

"Where do you live?" asked the operator.

Ole answered, "At the end of Eucalyptus Drive."

"Can you spell that for me?" the operator asked.

There was a long pause and finally Ole said, "How 'bout if I drag her over to Oak Street and you pick her up there?"

***

Ole is feeling down and goes to see a psychologist. He tells him, "Every morning, I wake up and look at my face in the mirror and it makes me want to vomit. What's wrong with me?"

The psychologist says, "I don't know, but we do know for sure that your eyesight is perfect."

***

At the marriage retreat, the instructor talked about the importance of knowing what matters to each other. "For example," he began, pointing to Ole, "do you know your wife's favorite flower?"

Ole answered, "Pillsbury All Purpose."

***

Ole went to the doctor for a physical. After Ole was dressed the doctor came in and said "I am sorry Ole, but you are very sick and have only a few weeks to live."

Ole went home with a heavy heart to tell Lena the news. After Ole told Lena he sat in his easy chair and Lena went to the kitchen. Soon a heavenly aroma came from the kitchen. Lena was making his favorite cookies! "Lena must really love me" he thought. Ole went into the kitchen and started to take a cookie. Lena slapped his hand away and said "Get away! These cookies aren't for you, they're for the funeral!"

***

Sven and Ole left Minnesota and went fishing in Canada. They returned with only one fish.

"The way I figure it, that fish cost us $2,000" said Sven.

"Well," said Ole, "At that price it's a good thing we didn't catch more."

***

Ole came home to find Lena dressed in a flimsy nightie, sitting on the bed with a bottle of champagne and the room filled with candles. Lena patted the bed and said "Ole come and sit by me." Ole sat down. Then Lena said "Ole I want you to make me feel like a real woman." Ole thought about it for a moment, stood up, and took off his shirt. He handed it to Lena and said "I need this ironed." His funeral is on Saturday.

***

Ole and Lena were visited by a door-to-door salesman, Lowell Thompson. He tried to convince them if they bought the freezer he was selling they would save enough on food bills to pay for the freezer. Ole responded that they were paying for the house on what they were saving on rent. And they were saving on movie tickets with the price of cable TV. Finally, Ole said, "And we're saving on laundry with the new washer and dryer. So, I guess we have to say, we can't afford to save any more right now."

***

Sven got a new truck so he called up Ole and says, "Ole, I got me a new truck! Do you want to go ice fishin' with me?"

"Sure!" says Ole.

So Ole went with Sven and Lena came along too to make sure there was no hanky-panky going on. Well Sven and Lena sat in the front seat and Ole sat back in the bed of the truck. They were on the lake when all of a sudden the truck went right through the ice!

Now even though Sven and Lena are pretty big people, they managed to get out of the truck, up to the surface, and back on top of the ice. They were waiting for Ole but he didn't show up. They were getting worried when he finally came up to the surface.

Sven says, "Ole what took you so long!"

"Well," says Ole, "It took me a while to figure out how to open the gate."

***

Ole and Sven were watching football and drinking beer when a commercial came on that said it could help men stay virile in their golden years.

"Ole," Sven said, "Am I in my golden years?"

"Not yet," Ole assured him. "But you sure are yellowing fast."

***

Sven is at the St. Gustav Cemetery and Hunting Lodge visiting the grave of his dearly departed mother. After a few minutes he places some

31

flowers on the ground and starts back towards his car when he sees another man kneeling at a grave. The man is praying with intense passion and keeps repeating, "Why did you have to die? Why did you have to die?"

Sven. feeling sorry for the man, goes over to him and says, "Sir, I don't want to interfere with your grieving, but this display of sadness is more then I've ever seen before. Who are you mourning? A child? A spouse? A parent?"

The mourner takes a moment to collect himself, then replies, "My wife's first husband."

***

Sven, Ole, and Lars were arrested in France during the French revolution. They each got to choose which way they would die. Sven chose the guillotine, because he saw it as the latest fashion. His head went under, but the blade stopped one inch from his neck. The French saw this as a sign from God or something and decided to let him go. The same thing happened to Lars. Then they asked Ole how he wanted to die he said "I think I'll take hanging, that guillotine doesn't work at all."

***

One particular Sunday Ole was lying back in the hammock and having just returned from church with Lena he was feeling a little religious. "God," said Ole, "when you made Lena, why did you make her so nice and round and so pleasant to hold?"

Suddenly a voice from above said, "So you would love her, Ole."

"Well then why, oh why," asked Ole, "why Lord did you make her so stupid?"

"So she would love you," replied the voice.

***

Ole was getting worried that Lena had a hearing problem. So one night when they were watching TV he called to her "What's for dinner Lena?" There was no response.

A minute later Ole asks again, this time louder "Lena, what's for dinner?" And again no response.

Finally Ole yells at the top of his lungs "What's for dinner Lena?"

Lena turns to him and says "For the third time, meatballs!"

***

Ole and Lena go to the fair and see a helicopter ride. Ole says, "Lena, I'm 85 years old. If I don't ride that helicopter now, I might not get another chance."

Lena angrily replies, "Ole that helicopter ride is fifty bucks, and fifty bucks is FIFTY BUCKS!"

The pilot overhears the couple and says, "Folks, I'll make you a deal. I'll take both of you for a ride. If you can stay quiet for the entire ride and don't say a word, I won't charge you a penny! But, if you say one word, it's fifty dollars."

Ole and Lena agree and up they go.

The pilot does all kinds of fancy maneuvers, but Ole and Lena don't say a word. He does his daredevil tricks over and over but they still don't say a word.

When they land, the pilot turns to Ole and says, "By golly, I did everything I could to make you yell out, but you didn't. I'm impressed!"

Ole replies, "Well, to tell you the truth, I almost said something when Lena fell out, but you know, fifty bucks is FIFTY BUCKS!"

*****

Ole and Lena got married. On their honeymoon trip they were nearing Minneapolis when Ole put his hand on Lena's knee. Giggling, Lena said, "Ole, you can go further than that if you want to." So Ole drove to Duluth.

*****

Sven was at the doctor for the seventh time in a month and each time he was told there was nothing wrong. The doctor came into the room and said, "Sven, I have good news and bad news." Sven said "Hmmmmm, tell me the good news first." So the doctor said "Well, Sven, you're not a hypochondriac after all."

***

Ole and Sven were drinking buddies who worked as aircraft mechanics in Minneapolis and one day the airport was fogged in and they were stuck in the hangar with nothing to do.

Ole said, "I wish we had somethin' to drink!"

Sven says, "Me too. Y'know, I hear you can drink that jet fuel and get a buzz. you wanna try it?"

So they pour themselves a couple of glasses of high octane hooch and got completely smashed.

Next morning Ole woke up and is surprised at how good he feels. In fact he feels GREAT! NO hangover! NO bad side effects. Nothing!

The phone rang. It was Sven who asks "How are you feelin' this morning?"

Ole says, "I feel great. How bout you?"

Sven says, "I feel great, too. You don't have no hangover?"

Ole says, "No that jet fuel is great stuff -- no hangover, nothing. We oughta do this more often."

Sven agreed. "Yeah, but there's just one ting."

Ole asked, "What's that?"

Sven questioned, "Have you farted yet?"

Ole stopped to think. "No "

"Well, DON'T, 'cause I'm in Iowa."

***

Ole was looking for a job and heard that there was an opening for a janitor at the local Lutheran church. He applied for the job and the interview went very well. "You have the job," he was told, "just sign this paper."

Ole made a big "X" on the paper.

"What's that?" he was asked.

"That's my mark."

"You're supposed to sign your name."

"That's my mark," Ole replied, "I can't read or write."

"What? We're sorry, but to work here you have to be able to sign your name."

Well, Ole finally got himself a job as a mate on a tugboat on the Mississippi, and eventually he became captain of his own tugboat. He did well for himself and eventually had a fleet of ships of his own and became one of the wealthiest men in the community.

One day the mayor decided to honor him for setting such a good example for others, and what they can accomplish with hard work and ingenuity. The mayor says, "Ole, we want to give you the key to the city! Just sign this form.

Ole made a big "X" on the paper.

"What's that?" he was asked.

"That's my mark."

"Your mark?" the mayor asked.

"Yah, I can't read or write, so that's my mark."

"You accomplished all of this not being able to read or write?" The mayor exclaimed. "Just think what you could have done if you could read and write!"

"Yah," Sven said. "I could've been a church janitor."

***

Lena and Hilda were at lunch. They started talking about keeping journals.

Hilda: "I write in my journal every night in a special book with a lock so Sven can't read it."

Lena: "I write my journal on the computer."

Hilda: "Wow, how do you keep Ole from reading your journal?"

Lena: "I put it in a file labeled 'Instruction Manuals.'"

***

Sven, Lars, and Ole die in a car accident and go to heaven. During their orientation, they are asked, "When you were in your casket, and friends and family were mourning over you, what would you have liked them to say about you?" Sven says, "I would've liked to hear them say, 'He was a good friend and a great family man.'" Lars says, "I would've liked to hear them say, 'He was a wonderful husband and a teacher who made a huge difference in many lives.'" Ole having heard what Sven and Lars said thought for a minute and said, "I would have liked to hear them say, 'Look, he's moving!'"

***

On Lena's birthday, Ole decided to wash the clothes for once to make her happy. Soon after entering the laundry room, he yelled, "Lena, what setting do I use on the washing machine?"

"It depends," Lena replied. "What does it say on your shirt?"

"University of Oslo." shouted Ole.

***

After 40 years of marriage, Ole and Lena found themselves in bed one night when Lena leaned over to Ole and said, "Ole, have you ever been unfaithful during all our years of marriage?"

"Not even once!" exclaimed Ole. "Lena, have you ever been unfaithful?" "Well, er, yes - but only three times," she admitted somewhat embarrassed.

"Hmmm, three times?" questioned Ole. "That's not so bad. Do you remember those three times? Can you tell me when?"

"Well Ole, do you remember when you wanted to build an addition, but had to get the okay from the building inspector?" she asked. "That was the first time."

"And do you remember when you wanted to build the store and you had a hard time getting approval from the president of the City Council?" asked Lena. "That was the second time."

"OK, Lena, when was the third time?" asked Ole?

"The third time was," Lena paused. "Do you remember when you were running for president of the Sons of Norway and you needed 125 votes?"

***

Lena is taking a shower when the doorbell rings. Ole, in the bathroom upstairs, yells for her to get the door. Lena throws a towel on and runs to open the door. Sven, their neighbor is there. Sven looks at Lena with only her towel on and says, "Lena if you drop the towel, I will give you five-hundred dollars."

So Lena drops her towel. Keeping his promise, Sven gives her the money and leaves. Lena closes the door and goes back to the bathroom. Ole asks her, "Who was that?

Lena replies, "Oh, that was Sven from next door." Lena thinks fast. "I don't know what he

wanted." Ole then asks, "Did he say anything about the five-hundred dollars he owes me?"

***

Sven took a trip to Fargo, North Dakota. While in a bar, a young woman on the next stool spoke to him in a friendly manner. "Look," she said, "let's play a game. I'll ask you a question and if you answer it correctly, I'll buy YOU a drink. But if you don't, then you buy ME a drink. Okay?"

"Yah, that sounds pretty good," said the Sven.

The woman said, "My father and mother had one child. It wasn't my brother. It wasn't my sister. Who was it?"

Sven scratched his head and finally said, "I give up. Who was it?"

"It was ME," laughed the woman.

So Sven paid for the drinks. Back in Minneapolis Sven went into a bar and spotted one of his best buddies, "Ole he said, "I got a game. If you can answer a question correctly, I'll buy you a drink. If you can't, then YOU have to buy ME one. Fair enough?"

"Fair enough," said Ole.

Okay . . . my father and mother had one child. It wasn't my brother, It wasn't my sister, Who was it?"

"Search me," said Ole. "I give up. Who was it?"
"It was some lady up in Fargo."

***

Ole and Sven were drinking at a bar in Brainerd, Minnesota.

Ole says, 'Did you know that lions have sex 10 to 15 times a night?'

'Darn!' says Sven. "I just joined the Elks."

***

Sven says to Ole "I found this pen, is it yours?"
Ole replies "I don't know, give it here"
He then tries it on a piece of paper and says "Yes it is"
Sven asks "How do you know?"
Ole replies, "That's my handwriting!"

***

Lars won a big lottery jackpot. He was asked to attend a press conference to announce his good luck.

"Will this change your life?" asked a reporter.

"Nah, I'll just do the same things I've always done," answered Lars.

Another reporter asked, "What about all of the letters begging for money?"

"Well," said Lars, "I'll keep sending them out just like usual."

***

A Mafia boss discovers that his bookkeeper, Sven, had stolen 10 million dollars from him. Sven is deaf—which is how he got the job in the first place; he would never hear anything that he'd have to testify about in court. When the boss confronts Sven about the missing money, he takes along his cousin Ole who knows sign language.

The boss says to Ole, "Ask him where my money is!" Using sign language, Ole delivers the boss's message.

Sven signs back, "I don't know what you're talking about."

Ole tells the Mafia boss, "He says he doesn't know what you're talking about."

The boss pulls out a pistol, puts it to Sven's head, and says, "Ask him again! If his memory doesn't improve he will be sleeping with the fishes."

Ole signs to the bookkeeper: "If you don't tell him, he'll kill you."

"OK. You win," Sven signs. "The money is in a suitcase, buried behind my Uncle Gustav's house!"

The mob boss asks, "What did he say?"

Ole replies "Nothing."

***

Ole was on his deathbed and implored his wife Lena, "Lena, when I'm gone, I want you to marry Sven Svenson."

"Why Sven Svenson?" Lena asked. "You've hated him all of your life!"

"Still do," gasped Ole.

***

Ole tried to sell his car. He was having a lot of problems selling it because the car had 250,000 miles on it.

One day, he told his problem to Sven who worked at the gas station. Sven told him, "Ole, there's a way to make the car easier to sell, but it ain't legal."

"That don't matter," replied Ole, "If I can sell the car, that's ok."

"Okay," said Sven. "Here's the address of a friend of mine. He owns a car repair shop. Tell him that Sven sent you and he will turn the counter in your car back to 50,000 miles. Then it won't be a problem to sell your car anymore."

The following weekend, Ole made the trip to the mechanic. About one month after that, Sven asked Ole, "Well Ole, did you sell your car?"

"No," replied Ole, "Why should I? Now it only has 50,000 miles on it."

***

Teacher: Little Ole, you missed school yesterday, didn't you?

Little Ole: Not very much.

***

Ole and Sven got a pilot to fly them to Canada to hunt deer. They bagged six. As they started loading the plane for the return trip, the pilot said the plane could take only four deer. Ole and Sven argued with the pilot, "Last year we shot six and the pilot let us put them all on board and he had the same plane as yours." Reluctantly, the pilot gave in and all six were loaded. However, even on full power, the little plane couldn't handle the load and went down a few moments after takeoff. Climbing out of the wreck Sven asked the Ole, "Any idea where we are?" Ole looked around and said, "Yah, I think were pretty close to where we crashed last year."

***

Lena: "Ole, if I die first, will you promise to ride to the cemetery with my mother?"

Ole: "Well, I suppose I can. But, I tell you . . . it will ruin my whole day."

***

Ole and Sven were at the movie theatre, and Sven bet that the hero would die during the movie. Ole didn't believe him, and they ended up betting $100 on it. When the movie was over and the hero was dead, Ole began to give the money to Sven, but Sven interrupted him "I already saw the movie, so I knew he was going to die. Keep the money." Ole replied, "Oh, I saw the movie before too, but I just didn't think he would be tricked twice."

***

Ole and Lena and Sven were out to dinner to celebrate Ole's 80th birthday. The waitress, who obviously didn't want a tip, said "Wow, 80 that's old." Ole snapped back "I may be old, in fact we all may be old, but we are still smart and sharp. Ask us a question."

So the waitress said, "How much is three squared?"

Sven quickly said "163."

Lena said, "Wrong it's Thursday!"

Ole shook his head and said "Nine"

The waitress asked how he knew the answer and he said "Well, I subtracted 163 from Thursday and got nine"

***

One day, Sven was walking down the street when who did he see driving a brand new Ford? It was Ole. Ole pulled up to him with a wide smile.

"Ole, where did you get that car?" Sven asked.

"Lena gave it to me."

"She gave it to you? I knew she was sweet on you, but this is incredible."

"Well, let me tell you what happened. We were driving out on County Road 17, in the middle of nowhere. Lena pulled off the road into the woods. She parked, got out of the car, took off all of her clothes and said, 'Ole take whatever you want.' So I took the car"

"Ole, you're a smart man, them clothes never would of fit you."

***

A distraught Ole phoned his doctor's office. "Is it true," he wanted to know, "that the pills you gave me have to be taken for the rest of my life?"

"Yes, I'm afraid so," the doctor told him. "Why do you ask?"

There was a moment of silence before the Ole replied, "I'm wondering, then, just how bad of shape am I in, 'cause the prescription is marked 'no refills.'"

***

Ole comes home unexpectedly at 3:00 in the afternoon.

Lena is lying naked on the bed

Ole "Lena what you doing, lying there naked on the bed"?

Lena "Ole I have nothing to wear."

Ole "What do you mean you have nothing to wear, you have a whole closet full of dresses."

Ole opens the closet door. "See, here's one dress, two dresses, three dresses, Hello Lars, four dresses, five dresses."

***

One day Ole was at the bar and talking with Sven, "I don't know what I should get Lena for our anniversary."

"Well, what did you get her last time?" Sven asked.

"I took her on a trip to Norway," answered Ole.

"Maybe you should take her on another trip," Sven said.

Ole thought for a while and then said, "That's the perfect gift! I'll send her a plane ticket so she can come back!"

***

Ole, a furniture dealer from up near Brainerd Minnesota, wanted to expand the line of furniture in his store, so he decided to go to Paris to see what he could find. After arriving in Paris he visited with some manufacturers and picked a line of furniture that he thought would sell well back home in Brainerd.

To celebrate the new line, he decided to visit a small cafe and have a glass of wine. As he sat enjoying his wine, he noticed that the place was quite crowded, and that the other chair at his table was the only vacant seat in the house. Before long, a very beautiful French woman came to his table, asked him something in French (which Ole couldn't understand), so he motioned to the vacant chair and invited her to sit down. He tried to talk to her but she didn't speak English so, after a couple of minutes of trying to communicate with her, he took a napkin and drew a picture of a wine glass and showed it to her. She nodded, so he ordered a glass of wine for her. After sitting together at the table for a while, he took another napkin, and drew a picture of a plate with food on it, and she nodded so they left the cafe and found a quiet place that featured a small group playing romantic music and ordered dinner. After eating he took another napkin and drew a picture of a couple dancing. She nodded, and they got up to dance. They danced until the cafe closed and the band was packing up. Back at their table, the young lady took a napkin and drew a picture of a four-poster bed. To this day, Ole has no idea how she figured out he was in the furniture business.

***

A reporter was interviewing a 103 year-old Lena: "And what do you think is the best thing about being 103?" the reporter asked. Lena simply replied, "No peer pressure."

***

Sven came home from work early one day and Lena asks, "Sven, you're home from work early. What happened?"

Sven replies, "Well, I got my thing caught in the pickle slicer."

"Oh no!." says Lena, "Let me see your thing."

So Sven shows her his thing and everything is fine.

"Sven, your thing is just fine, what happened to the pickle slicer?"

Says Sven, "Oh they fired her too."

***

Sven and Ole decided to open a bungee-jump concession down in Mexico. On opening day, a large crowd gathered at the base of the bungee-jump tower. However no one bought a ticket.

Sven and Ole were standing on the top of the bungee tower. Ole asked," Why isn't anyone buying a ticket?" Sven answered, "Maybe they don't understand what a bungee-jump is. Why don't you make a jump to show them how it works."

So Ole attached the bungee-cords and jumped. He returned to the platform with a torn shirt, and bloody arms.

Not knowing what happened, Sven told Ole to try again. And again he jumped and returned more beat up than before.

Sven asked Ole, "What happened?"

Ole replied, "I don't know but what's a piñata?"

***

Ole went in to see the minister at St. Olav Lutheran Church. "Reverend Johnson, my wife Lena is trying to poison me."

Reverend Johnson said "Why don't you let me talk to her and find out what is happening."

The next day Ole got a call from Reverend Johnson "Ole, I spoke to Lena for four hours this morning. I suggest you take the poison."

***

Sven and Ole go to the beach, and after a couple hours Sven says, "This isn't fun. How come the girls aren't friendly to me?"

"Well, I tell you, Sven, maybe if you put a potato in your swim trunks that would help."

So Sven does, but he comes back to Ole later, and he says, "I tried what you told me with the potato, but it doesn't help."

Ole looked at him and said "No, Sven --- you're supposed to put the potato in the front."

***

One day Lena stops Ole and tells him that the outhouse is full and he has to do something about it. Ole says that Sven is coming over next weekend, and since he has been going to engineering school he might have an idea of the best way to handle the situation.

That weekend Sven comes over and Ole explains his dilemma. "Sven, we got to do somethin' about the outhouse, it is full and Lena is getting upset about it."

"Well Ole, I have an idea. We will place several sticks of dynamite around the outside of the outhouse with a fuse just long enough to allow us to run behind the house before it goes off. The outhouse will be blown straight up, the crap in the hole will be blown out into the fields to fertilize them, then the outhouse will fall right back down to where it was."

Ole thought this was a fantastic plan so he and Sven got to work and set all the dynamite just right. They lit the fuse and ran for the house. Just as they got to the back of the house Lena came running out the back door and made a beeline for the outhouse. Before Ole could stop her she ducked into the outhouse slamming the door behind her and BOOOOM!, the dynamite blew the outhouse straight up in the air, the crap was blown out into the fields, and then the outhouse dropped right back down where it originally sat, just like Sven had planned.

Ole runs to the outhouse worried about Lena and reaches it just as she opens the door to come out. "Lena, Lena.....are you alright?"

Lena is a little shaken up but responds "Yes Ole, I am fine but I have to tell you, I'm sure glad I didn't let that one go in the house!"

***

Little Sven and Little Ole are walking through the woods one day when they spy some rabbit droppings. Little Sven says, "Hey, what are those things?"

"I think they are smart pills," say Little Ole. "Eat some of 'em and it'll make you smarter."

So Little Sven eats some of them and says, "Uff da...these taste like crap."

"See," Little Ole replies. "You're gettin' smarter already."

***

Lena asks Ole, "Ole if I were to die first, would you remarry?"

"Well," says Ole, "I'm in good health, so why

54

not?"

"Would she live in my house?" asks Lena

"It's all paid up, so yes," replies Ole.

"Would she drive my car?"

"It's new, so yes."

"Would she use my golf-clubs?"

"No. She's left-handed."

***

Little Ole: My teacher was mad at me because I didn't know where the Rockies were.

Lena: Well, next time remember where you put things!

***

Ole tells Sven, "I've been in love with the same woman for 25 years now Sven."

Sven replies, "Ole that's wonderful!"

Ole gets a serious look before he replies, "Yah, but if my wife Lena finds out, she'll kill me."

***

Ole was having lunch with Sven when he said "I'm a little worried about Lena. I think she has a few screws loose." Sven says "What makes you think that?" "Well," Ole replied, "It's a lot of things like today she is going to the store to return a scarf I bought for her." Sven shrugs his shoulders "So what's wrong with that?" Ole shook his head and said "She claims it was too tight."

***

As Sven approached his neighbor Ole's barn, he saw Ole singing to his tractor, paying it compliments, and dancing around it suggestively.

"What are you doing?" Sven asked.

Ole replied, "Me and Lena been having um, marital difficulties, and the marriage counselor said I needed to do somethin' sexy to a tractor."

***

Lena was arrested for shoplifting in a supermarket near Madelia, Minnesota. When she went before the judge he asked her, "What did you steal?'

Lena replied, "A can of peaches."

The judge asked her how many peaches were in the can.

She replied "There were six."

The judge said, 'Then I will give you six days in jail."

Before the judge could actually pronounce the punishment, Ole stood up, and asked the judge if he could say something. The judge said, "What is it?"

Ole said, "She also stole a can of peas."

***

Ole and Sven were camping one weekend and went walking through the woods when they suddenly see a huge brown bear in the clearing ahead. The bear sees them too and begins to head towards them.

Ole quickly digs a pair of sneakers out of his backpack and frantically begins to put them on.

"What the heck are you doin?" asks Sven. "Them sneakers ain't gonna help you outrun a bear."

Ole continues to put on his sneakers "I don't need to outrun that bear," he replies. "I just need to outrun you."

***

Ole goes into the Social Security Office and fills out an application. Too old to have a birth certificate, he is asked to prove he is old enough. He opens his shirt and shows them the gray hair on his chest and they accept that as proof.

Ole then goes home to Lena, shows her the check, and explains to her what has happened. Lena replies, "Well get back down there, pull down your pants, and see if you can get disability!"

***

Ole was driving home from work when he was pulled over for speeding. Two days later he was given another ticket by the same officer for speeding on the same road.

"So," the officer asked, "Ole, have you learned anything today?!" Ole said. "Yah, I learned I need to take a different way home from work!"

***

Ole and Lena went to the same Lutheran Church. Ole went on Christmas and Easter and once in awhile, he went on one of the other Sundays. Lena went every Sunday and taught Sunday School. On one of those Sundays when Ole was there he sat in the pew next to Lena and noticed she was a nice looking woman.

While they were taking the collection, as Ole handed the collection to plate to her he said, "Hey, Lena, how about you and me go to dinner in New Prague next Friday?"

"Yah, Ole, that would be nice," said Lena.

Well, Ole couldn't believe his luck. All week long he polished up his old Chevy, and on Friday he picked Lena up and took her to the finest restaurant in New Prague.

When they sat down, Ole looked over at Lena and said, "Hey, Lena, would you like a cocktail before dinner?"

"Oh, no, Ole," said Lena. "What would I tell my Sunday School class?"

Well, Ole was set back a bit, so he didn't say much until after dinner. Then he reached in his

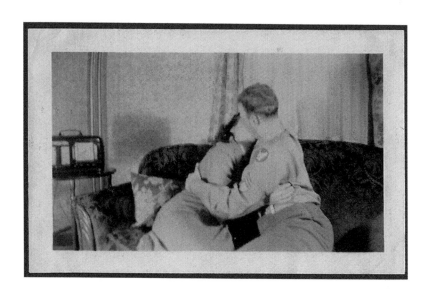

pocket and pulled out a pack of cigarettes. "Hey, Lena," said Ole, "would you like a smoke?"

"Oh, no, Ole," said Lena. "What would I tell my Sunday School class?"

Well, Ole was feeling pretty low after that, so he just got in his Chevy and was driving Lena home when they passed the Riverside Motel. He'd already struck out twice so he figured he had nothing to lose.

"Hey, Lena," said Ole, "how would you like to stop at that motel with me?"

"Yah, Ole, that would be nice," said Lena.

Well, Ole couldn't believe his luck. He did a U-turn right there in the middle of the highway, drove across the median, drove back to the motel, and checked in with Lena and they spent the night doing, well you know.

The next morning Ole got up first. He looked at Lena lying there in the bed, her tousled hair on the pillow.

"What have I done? thought Ole.

He woke Lena up. "Lena, I've got to ask you something," said Ole. "What're you going to tell your Sunday School class?"

"Lena said, "The same thing I always tell them. You don't have to smoke and drink to have a good time!"

***

Little Sven invited his mother Helga over for dinner. During the meal, Helga couldn't help noticing how beautiful Little Sven's roommate Inga was. She had been suspicious of what was going on between Little Sven and Inga and this only made her more curious. During dinner, watching the two of them, Helga started to wonder if her suspicions were true.

Reading his mom's thoughts, Little Sven volunteered, "I know what you must be thinkin' mom, but Inga and I are just roommates."

About a week later, Inga told Little Sven, "Ever since your mother was here, I can't find the silver gravy ladle. You don't suppose she took it?"

Little Sven said, "Hmmmmmm, I doubt it, but I'll e-mail her just to be sure."

"Dear Mom," he wrote, "I'm not sayin' you took a gravy ladle from my house, and I'm not saying you didn't take a gravy ladle, but the truth is that the silver gravy ladle has been missing since you were here last week for dinner. Did you, for some reason, take it with you?"

A few days later, Little Sven received a reply from Helga: "Dear Son, I'm not saying that you do sleep with Inga, and I'm not saying that you don't sleep with Inga, but the truth is that if she were sleepin' in her own bed, she'd have found the gravy ladle by now. Love, Mom."

***

Lena and Helga walk into a tanning salon. The receptionist asks, "Are you two sisters?" Lena laughed and said, " No, we aren't even Catholic."

***

Sven and Ole got a job putting in telephone poles. After the first day, they were talking to the foreman. The foreman asked how many poles they had put in.

"Two" said Ole.

"Only TWO?" asked the foreman, "All the other crews put in eight to ten."

"Yah!" Said Ole, "But did you see how much they left sticking out?"

***

Sven and Ole decide one day to enter thoroughbred horse racing, and they each go out and buy a horse. Unfortunately, they only have enough money left afterward to rent one stable.

"Uff dah, Sven," said Ole, "With both our horses in one stable, how will we tell them apart?"

Sven says, "I got an idea." He grabs a bucket of red paint and paints a big X on the side of his horse.

"Yah sure," says Ole, "That'll work just fine."

But when they go to reclaim their horses from the stable after the first race, the horse's sweat had completely washed the red X away, and they

62

spent hours arguing over which horse belongs to who.

Once they sorted their horses out again, Sven says to Ole, "Well? You got any bright ideas?"

"Yah sure," says Ole, and he cuts his horse's tail very short. "There. Now we can tell."

And, in fact, the idea works just fine, until Ole's horse's tail grew back out, and they got their horse's confused again. After a good rousing fist fight, they get everything straightened out.

"We need a good way to tell them darn things apart," says Ole, nursing a black eye.

"Yah sure," says Sven, "But what?"

They sit and think for a long time, and then suddenly Ole bursts to his feet. He runs off, and returns a few minutes later with a measuring tape. He measures one horse and then the other.

Sven asks, "Will it work?"

Ole proudly exclaims, "Yah sure Sven! The black horse is four inches shorter than the brown one!"

***

So Ole won the door prize at Sons of Norway a while back. It was a brand new toilet brush that the Ace hardware had donated. Ole was really happy about winning, he talked about it all night. Said he never had ever won anything before. He took it home and tried it out right away and he give it a good trial. But after a couple weeks he figured he'd go back to using paper.

***

Ole and Lars were working for the city public works department in Wisconsin. Ole would dig a hole and Lars would follow behind and fill the hole in. They worked up one side of the street, then down the other, then moved on to the next street, working furiously all day without rest, one digging a hole, the other filling it in again.

An onlooker was amazed at their hard work, but couldn't understand what they were doing. So he asked Ole, 'I'm impressed by the effort you two are putting in to your work, but I don't get it -- why do you dig a hole, only to have your partner follow behind and fill it up again?'

Ole wiped his brow and sighed, 'Well, I suppose it probably looks odd because we're normally a three-person team. But today Sven, who plants the trees called in sick.'

***

Ole and Lena were sitting in the living room. Ole turns to Lena says, "Just so you know, I never want to live in a vegetative state dependent on some machine. If that ever happens, just pull the plug." Lena nods, gets up, and unplugs the TV.

***

Ole and Sven were at the bar. Ole was walking kind of funny so Sven asked, "Hey Ole why are you walking so funny?" Ole responded "I had a vasectomy yesterday and I'm kind of sore." Well Sven is shocked – they are both in the 70s as are their wives so he says "Why would you have a vasectomy at this age?" Ole took a gulp of his beer and said "I don't want any more grandchildren."

***

Ole: You want to go for a walk?
Sven: Isn't it windy?
Ole: No, it's Thursday.
Sven: Me, too. Let's go get a beer.

***

Ole and Sven were police officers and one night they were both working – Ole was out patrolling the neighborhood and Sven was back at the station monitoring calls. All of a sudden Sven hears Ole on the radio.

"'This is Ole callin' in, Ole callin' in. Come in please."

Sven replies "What is it Ole? this is Sven. You sound upset."

"Yah I am that," Ole said, "A lady just shot her husband for steppin' on the floor she just mopped."

"Well you gotta arrest her and bring her in," Sven answered.

"Well I can't," Ole said.
"Why, not?"
"The floor's still wet."

***

Ole wasn't feeling well so he went to the doctor. After examining him the doctor took his wife, Lena, aside, and said, "Your husband has a very sensitive heart. I am afraid he's not going to make it, unless you treat him like a king, which means you are at his every beck and call, 24 hours a day, seven days a week, and make sure that he doesn't have to do anything himself."

On the way home Ole asked with a note of concern "What did the doctor say to you?

"Well," Lena responded, "he said it looks like you probably won't make it."

***

Ole and Sven are sitting in a bar. Suddenly, a couple of robbers walk in and shout, "This is a holdup!" As the thieves move from customer to customer relieving them of their wallets and jewelry, Ole slips Sven a wad of cash and whispers, "Here's that hundred I owe you."

***

"I wonder what time it is?" Ole asked Sven.

"I don't have a watch but I know it's not 9:00," Sven answered.

Ole says "Well if you don't have a watch how do you know it's not 9:00?"

Sven replied "Because at 9:00 I'm supposed to be home, and I'm not home now."

***

One day Ole and Sven had been on a boat when it sank so they were now in a life raft on Lake Superior. It would soon be dark and there were no other boats nearby. While looking through the boat's provisions, Ole found an old lamp.

He rubbed the lamp and suddenly, a genie popped out. This genie, however, stated that he could only grant one wish, not the usual three.

Without thinking, or consulting Sven, Ole immediately blurted out, "Turn the entire lake into Hamm's beer".

The genie clapped his hands and immediately Lake Superior turned into Hamm's beer and the genie immediately vanished.

Now only the sound of beer lapping on the side of the life raft could be heard as Ole and Sven pondered their new situation.

Sven looked at Ole whose wish had been granted, and after a period of long tension-filled silence, Sven said, "Nice going Ole! Now we're going to have to pee in the boat."

***

Mary E. Hirsch

The End

Made in the USA
Las Vegas, NV
25 October 2020

10314606R10039